THE NBA

A HISTORY OF HOOPS

Published by Creative Education
P.O. Box 227, Mankato, Minnesota 56002
Creative Education is an imprint of The Creative Company
www.thecreativecompany.us

Design and production by Christine Vanderbeek
Art direction by Rita Marshall

Printed by Corporate Graphics in the United States of America

Photographs by Corbis (Bettmann, Steve Lipofsky), Dreamstime (Munktcu),
Getty Images (Andrew D. Bernstein/NBAE, Nathaniel S. Butler/NBAE, Cameron
Davidson, James Drake/Sports Illustrated, Stephen Dunn, Focus On Sport, FPG,
Glenn James/NBAE, George Long/Sports Illustrated, Chris McGrath, Fernando
Medina/NBAE, NBA Photos/NBAE, Ken Regan/NBAE, Wen Roberts/NBAE,
Ragnar Schmuck, Carl Skalak/Sports Illustrated, SM/AIUEO), iStockphoto
(Brandon Laufenberg)

Library of Congress Cataloging-in-Publication Data
Goodman, Michael E.
The story of the New York Knicks / by Michael E. Goodman.
p. cm. — (The NBA: a history of hoops)
Includes index.
Summary: The history of the New York Knicks professional basketball team from
its start in 1946 to today, spotlighting the franchise's greatest players and reliving
its most dramatic moments.
ISBN 978-1-58341-955-7
1. New York Knickerbockers (Basketball team)—History—Juvenile literature.
2. Basketball—New York (State)—New York—Juvenile literature. I. Title. II. Series.
GV885.52.N4G67 2009   796.323'64'097471—dc22   2009035974

CPSIA: 120109 PO1093

First Edition
2 4 6 8 9 7 5 3 1

Page 3: Forward Wilson Chandler
Pages 4–5: Guard Nate Robinson

THE STORY OF THE

NEW YORK
KNICKS

MICHAEL E. GOODMAN

CREATIVE ● EDUCATION

CONTENTS

CHAPTER ONE

THE KNICKS HAVE CLASS

In 1626, a group of Dutch colonists established the settlement of New Amsterdam on a small island along the middle Atlantic coast. Those settlers wore special knee-length pants called "knickerbockers," or "knickers" for short. Even after the colony passed into British hands and was renamed New York, the term "Knickerbockers" was still used to describe residents who traced their ancestry back to the original Dutch settlers. In the 1800s, a figure called "Father Knickerbocker" became a popular symbol of New York City in political cartoons.

Knickerbockers took on a new meaning in 1946 when a professional league called the Basketball Association of America (BAA) was founded. The owners of the New York franchise needed to pick a name for their club, so each person printed a name onto a slip of paper and put it in a hat. As it turned out, nearly every slip read "Knickerbockers." The name was quickly shortened to "Knicks" by sportswriters to save space in sports page headlines.

The Knicks' home arena, the famous Madison Square Garden, is located amid the towering skyscrapers of the bustling borough of Manhattan.

IN 1950, THREE YEARS AFTER JACKIE ROBINSON BROKE MAJOR LEAGUE BASEBALL'S COLOR BARRIER, THE KNICKS BECAME THE FIRST NBA TEAM TO SIGN AN AFRICAN AMERICAN PLAYER—FORWARD NAT "SWEETWATER" CLIFTON. The 6-foot-7 Chicago native, whose nickname was derived from his love of soft drinks, had come to the Knicks' attention while performing with the Harlem Globetrotters in the late 1940s. Clifton's huge hands enabled him to snare one-handed rebounds and whip outlet passes to teammates heading downcourt. When he first joined the Knicks, Clifton seemed almost too mild-mannered for New York coach Joe Lapchick. Then, during a preseason game in 1951, a Boston Celtics player shoved Clifton and shouted a racial slur at him. The Knicks forward decked the loudmouthed opponent and offered to take on the entire Boston team. The incident seemed to awaken an aggressive instinct in Clifton and earned him respect around the league. While he was an integral part of the Knicks squad on the court, Clifton was still not allowed to stay at the same hotel as his teammates during road trips to several southern and midwestern cities.

COURTSIDE STORIES

"SWEETWATER" MAKES HISTORY

Nat "Sweetwater" Clifton in 1950.

The Knicks established a reputation as being one of the classiest teams in the BAA as well as the National Basketball Association (NBA), which was formed three years later. Ned Irish, the club's founder, had a clear-cut philosophy: "We will create first-class conditions for a first-class team in a first-class city," he declared. Thanks to Irish, the Knicks boasted professional basketball's first training camp, its first athletic trainer, and its most aggressive scouting program. Irish also found a first-class coach to lead his new squad—Joe Lapchick, who left nearby St. John's University to take over the local pro team.

Lapchick's reputation as a basketball mentor helped him draw top young talent to the Knicks. In 1947, for example, guard Carl Braun—an outstanding baseball and basketball prospect—decided to break his pitching contract with the New York Yankees for the chance to play basketball under Lapchick. Braun was noted for the deadly accurate two-handed set shot that he released from over his head. He would put up dozens of shots in practice, often whispering "swish" as the ball sailed through the net. A Knicks radio broadcaster overheard the new word and became the first to use it on the air.

While Braun was the team's brightest star, the entire club formed a well-balanced constellation. "Everyone knew his role," said center Harry Gallatin. "Dicky McGuire was the playmaker, Carl [Braun] was the shooter, Ernie Vandeweghe did damage in a kind of all-around way, and

Nat [Clifton] and I would sweep the boards, outlet the ball, and run. We played true team ball. Coach Lapchick wouldn't have had it any other way."

apchick's Knicks quickly rose toward the top of the NBA's Eastern Division, even though no starter was taller than 6-foot-6. They relied on crisp passing, strong rebounding, and solid defense. The Knicks were especially tough at playoff time. They reached the division finals four years in a row (1950–53) and played in three straight NBA Finals in 1951, 1952, and 1953. However, they were never quite able to win a championship.

Then age began to slow down some of the Knicks' best players. Starting with the 1956–57 season, New York finished last in its division 9 out of the next 10 years and made the playoffs just once. Talented players such as forwards Kenny Sears and Willie Naulls and guard Richie Guerin led the Knicks during much of this down period, but they never achieved success as a unit.

HARRY GALLATIN

POSITION FORWARD / CENTER
HEIGHT 6-FOOT-6
KNICKS SEASONS 1948–57

THE KNICKS' FIRST-EVER DRAFT PICK IN 1948, HARRY GALLATIN WAS THE TEAM'S CORNERSTONE FOR NEARLY A DECADE. Gallatin's nickname was "Harry the Horse" because he was so strong. Knicks fans also called him "Mr. Inside" because of his importance to the team near the basket. The 6-foot-6 Gallatin out-rebounded players many inches taller than he because, as Knicks forward Vince Boryla noted, "he was simply too stubborn to let an opponent get a rebound." Gallatin led the league in rebounding in 1953–54. Even more impressive was the fact that he never missed a game during his NBA career. In fact, Gallatin often proudly boasted that he had never missed a practice or a game in high school, college, or the pros. A seven-time All-Star during his playing days, Gallatin coached both NBA and college teams following his pro career. He was named NBA Coach of the Year in 1963 when he took the St. Louis Hawks to the Western Division finals. Harry the Horse was inducted into the Basketball Hall of Fame in 1991.

CHAPTER TWO

REBUILDING WITH RED AND REED

In late 1966, Knicks management, hoping to reverse the team's losing trend, hired William "Red" Holzman as coach. A native New Yorker, Holzman had been an outstanding player in the early days of the NBA, and he had served as the Knicks' top scout for a decade before becoming their coach. Holzman believed strongly that, for a club to win, individuals had to be willing to sacrifice some of their own statistics for the good of the team.

Under Holzman's direction as scout and coach, the Knicks drafted and traded for a remarkable group of team-oriented players. First, there was center Willis Reed, the club's captain and inspirational leader. The 6-foot-9 Reed was wide and strong, and he had the heart to outbattle bigger players. Reed began his Knicks career out of position as a power forward, with 6-foot-11 giant Walt Bellamy as the team's center. However, when Bellamy showed little interest in playing defense,

Willis Reed was an immediate star, scoring 46 points in 1 game his first season to help clinch the 1965 NBA Rookie of the Year award.

AMONG THE RETIRED NUMBERS HANGING FROM THE RAFTERS OF NEW YORK'S MADISON SQUARE GARDEN IS AN UNUSUAL BANNER BEARING THE NAME "HOLZMAN" AND THE NUMBER 613. The banner honors William "Red" Holzman, the winningest coach in franchise history, and "613" represents the total number of victories his teams achieved during his 14 seasons as Knicks head coach. When a writer once called Holzman a "genius," the court general gruffly replied, "I don't think there is such a thing as a coaching genius, just a hard worker." Holzman pushed his players hard and demanded that they tame their egos and devote all of their energy to playing together as a smooth-running unit. He seldom smiled on the sidelines but almost never raised his voice, either. "Red tries to give one the impression that he's a hard, rough, impersonal coach," said team captain and center Willis Reed. "He's really just a pussycat with more knowledge of basketball than any man I've ever known." During the NBA's 50th anniversary celebration in 1996, Holzman was named one of the league's top 10 coaches of all time.

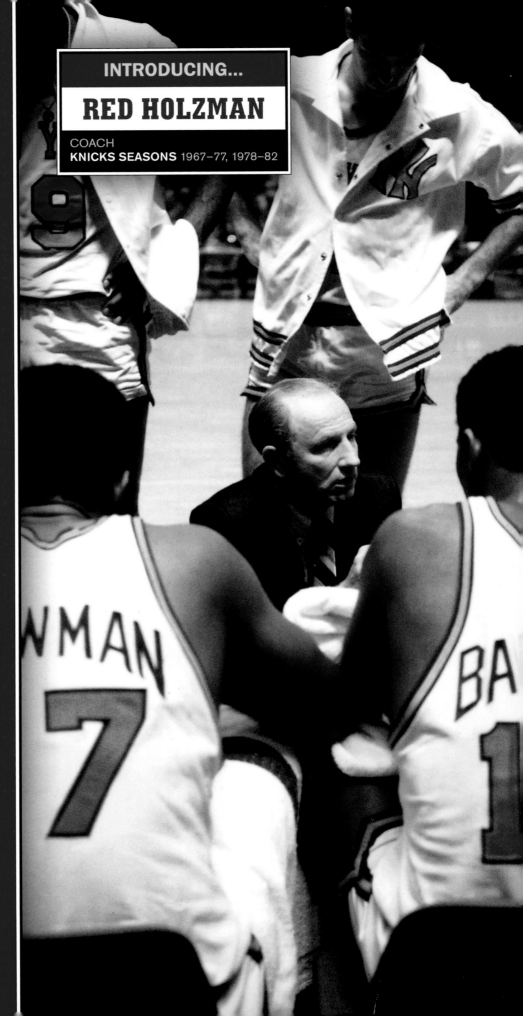

INTRODUCING...

RED HOLZMAN

COACH
KNICKS SEASONS 1967–77, 1978–82

Holzman engineered a trade with the Detroit Pistons for forward Dave DeBusschere, an outstanding rebounder and defender. The third front-court player was Bill Bradley, who ran tirelessly around the court looking to unleash his deadly outside shot.

The team's starting backcourt consisted of Walt Frazier, a flashy guard who was both an offensive threat and defensive stalwart, and Dick Barnett, an outstanding clutch performer. Coming off the bench were long-range bomber Cazzie Russell and defensive specialist Phil Jackson, a gangly forward who would later become one of the NBA's most successful coaches.

Holzman molded these individuals into an outstanding two-way unit. "I stressed defense—pressure defense—and team basketball. And, on offense, moving the ball to hit the open man," Holzman explained. Holzman had a somewhat crusty and dictatorial manner, but his players always respected him. "Playing basketball [under Holzman] became more fun than I had ever imagined," said Bradley.

H olzman's team reached its peak in 1969–70, winning a club-record 60 games and storming through the first 2 rounds of the playoffs. For the fourth time in their history, the Knicks prepared to battle for an NBA title. Their opponents were the Los Angeles Lakers, led by future Hall-of-Famers Wilt Chamberlain, Jerry West, and Elgin Baylor. The teams split the first four games, with two going into overtime. New York then won Game 5 but lost Reed when the captain tore a thigh muscle driving to the basket and had to be carried off the court. With Reed out, Chamberlain easily dominated Game 6, reducing the series to a one-game showdown.

HARD WORK CAME NATURALLY TO WILLIS REED. Born in rural Louisiana, Reed began picking cotton at age nine to help support his family. By ninth grade, he split his time between attending high school, playing basketball, and working alongside grown men in a wheat storehouse. Later, at Grambling College, Reed earned a reputation as a tireless rebounder with a soft touch from the outside. The Knicks made him their second pick in the 1964 NBA Draft, and he had an immediate impact, leading the club in scoring and rebounding his rookie year. Reed set many team records during his 10 seasons with the Knicks. He also was named to seven NBA All-Star teams and earned league Most Valuable Player (MVP) honors in 1970. Coach Red Holzman named Reed team captain, and he took the role very seriously, pushing the veterans and encouraging the younger players. "He made you understand that you were very lucky to play in this league," said forward Mel Davis, "but if you worked long and hard on your skills, you would have a prosperous career."

INTRODUCING...

WILLIS REED

POSITION CENTER
HEIGHT 6-FOOT-9
KNICKS SEASONS 1964–74

BILL BRADLEY WAS A TWO-TIME NBA CHAMPION WITH THE KNICKS. Yet his life's highlights included much more than basketball. Bright and hardworking, Bradley was an Eagle Scout, studied at the prestigious University of Oxford on a Rhodes Scholarship, and served six months in the Air Force Reserve. He also came up with unique workouts to make himself a better athlete, such as putting weights in his shoes and then jumping for extended periods. Only after all that did he suit up for the Knicks for 11 seasons, averaging 12.4 points a game on some star-studded rosters and playing with such savvy and determination that he was later inducted into the Hall of Fame despite his relatively modest statistics. Bradley retired in 1977, but only seven months later, he embarked on a new challenge, winning a seat as a United States senator for the state of New Jersey. Bradley put the same passion that had made him a hoops star into his political career, earning reelection to the Senate twice and even campaigning for the U.S. presidency in 2000.

COURTSIDE STORIES

LIFE BEYOND BASKETBALL

Bill Bradley beats a defender.

Just before Game 7 began, Reed decided to play despite the pain. He announced the decision to his teammates, who were thrilled. "It was like getting your left arm sewed back on," said Russell. The hometown fans in Madison Square Garden went wild as Reed limped onto the court for the opening tip-off. In their hearts, the game and the championship were already won. Reed scored only four points early in the game, but he played tough defense against Chamberlain. Just having him on the court inspired his teammates and the fans as the Knicks earned a 113–99 victory. Of course, it didn't hurt that Frazier had the game of his life, scoring 36 points and handing out 19 assists. Finally, after 23 years, the Knickerbockers were champs at last!

Three years later, the Knicks won a second league title with a slightly different cast. Barnett had been replaced in the starting lineup by high-scoring guard Earl "The Pearl" Monroe, one of the most creative offensive players in NBA history. The Frazier–Monroe backcourt tandem directed another balanced New York attack and propelled the Knicks over the Lakers once again for the 1973 championship.

WALT FRAZIER BECAME A LEGEND IN NEW YORK FOR HIS STYLE BOTH ON THE BASKETBALL COURT AND OFF IT. Frazier was nicknamed "Clyde" by his teammates, after Warren Beatty's stylish character in the movie *Bonnie and Clyde*. When he wasn't thrilling fans in Madison Square Garden, Frazier loved being seen outside New York's poshest clubs, driving his Rolls-Royce "Clyde-mobile" and wearing a long fur coat and floppy fedora hat. A seven-time NBA All-Star, Frazier was nearly as exciting to watch when he played defense as when he was scoring or handing out assists on offense. Quick hands, catlike reflexes, and great court awareness helped Frazier earn a spot on the NBA's All-Defensive squad 7 times in his 10 seasons in New York. He was inducted into the Basketball Hall of Fame in 1987. Following his playing career, Frazier joined the Knicks' radio and television broadcast teams, where his love of big words and colorful rhymes—such as "dishing and swishing," "hustle and muscle," or "flexing and vexing"—earned him a new set of fans.

Dave DeBusschere rebounds versus the Lakers in the 1973 playoffs.

A PERFECT SEVEN

IN APRIL 1973, ON THE WAY TO THEIR SECOND NBA TITLE, THE KNICKS HAD ONE MAJOR OBSTACLE TO OVERCOME IN THE EASTERN CONFERENCE FINALS—THEIR FIERCEST RIVALS, THE BOSTON CELTICS, WINNER OF 11 LEAGUE CHAMPIONSHIPS. Led by swingman John Havlicek and center Dave Cowens, the Celtics finished far ahead of the Knicks during the regular season and were heavily favored to beat out New York for a spot in the NBA Finals. Unintimidated, the Knicks blew out the Celtics in Game 2 and captured the next two contests to take a commanding three-games-to-one series lead. Then Boston staged exciting fourth-quarter comebacks in Games 5 and 6 to set up a winner-take-all battle in Game 7 at Boston Garden. The Celtics had never lost a Game 7 in a playoff series, at home or on the road, but the Knicks were surprisingly confident. "I just never had any doubts we'd win, and I'm not that way," said New York coach Red Holzman. The Knicks fell behind early on but used a stifling pressure defense to key a 94–78 victory and continue their championship run.

CHAPTER THREE

FROM KING TO EWING

Over the next few years, core members of the Knicks' title clubs aged and lost some of their edge. They were replaced by such talented newcomers as guards Ray Williams and Micheal Ray Richardson and center Bill Cartwright, but these new Knicks were unable to match the "team" play of Holzman's champs. After the Knicks stumbled to a 33–49 record in 1981–82, the legendary coach also decided to retire.

Holzman was replaced by Hubie Brown, a demanding leader who required his club to run a patterned offense and press and trap continuously on defense. It took the players a while to adapt to this new style, but they finally succeeded. One key to their success was the play of forward Bernard King, who arrived in New York in 1982. A fierce competitor, the 6-foot-7 King could score consistently from the outside, but his specialty was driving inside, using his speed and

Before Patrick Ewing arrived, Bill Cartwright (pictured) manned the post in New York for six seasons, earning All-Star honors as a rookie.

agility to leave defenders behind. "He's like a bird," said Coach Brown. "He swoops toward the basket and seems to be descending. Then, at the last instant, he elevates, and you'll see an incredible move."

King scored nearly 22 points per game in his first season in New York. Then he really found his offensive touch, averaging 26.3 points per game in 1983–84 and leading the NBA with a 32.9 average the next season. Stingy defense and King's scoring propelled the club to the playoffs in both 1983 and 1984. Unfortunately, the Knicks came to rely too heavily on King for their offensive power. When the star forward suffered a devastating knee injury late in the 1984–85 season and was lost for nearly two years, New York quickly sank in the standings.

DUEL IN DETROIT

Isiah Thomas shoots over Bernard King (number 30).

BASKETBALL IS A TEAM SPORT, BUT THE FINAL GAME OF A FIRST-ROUND 1984 PLAYOFF SERIES BETWEEN THE KNICKS AND DETROIT PISTONS TURNED INTO AN AMAZING ONE-ON-ONE DUEL BETWEEN KNICKS FORWARD BERNARD KING AND PISTONS GUARD ISIAH THOMAS.

The battle took place in Detroit's Joe Louis Arena, where a defective heating system had players and fans sweating. King had averaged 40 points per game during the first 4 contests, and he was just as effective in Game 5. The Knicks led by 8 points with less than 2 minutes remaining when Thomas took over and scored a remarkable 16 points in 94 seconds! Still, King, playing with dislocated fingers on both hands, offset Thomas's efforts with timely baskets of his own, and the game went into overtime. With the Knicks leading by just two points in overtime, King soared far above the basket to slam home a rebound and secure the series victory for New York. "I probably never jumped that high before in my life," King later told reporters. By game's end, King had outscored Thomas 44–33 in a duel that became an NBA legend.

B ut there was a silver lining to the Knicks' dark cloud of bad luck. Thanks to its low finish in 1984–85, New York was awarded the top pick in the 1985 NBA Draft. With it, Knicks management chose the player who would be the heart of the team for the next 15 years—center Patrick Ewing. "The Patrick Ewing Era Has Begun," announced a May 13, 1985, headline in *The New York Times*.

An outstanding defender and scorer at Georgetown University, Ewing had led the Hoyas to three college national championship games, and the Knicks were counting on the seven-footer to take them to glory as well. Ewing was a dominant presence in the paint and boasted a deadly fadeaway jump shot. He also had a brooding "game face" that intimidated opponents. Still, the Ewing Era got off to a rocky start. It took several years—and several coaching changes—before the Knicks were able to surround their powerful center with the right supporting players. This lineup included point guard Mark Jackson, bruising forwards Charles Oakley and Anthony Mason, and guards John Starks and Gerald Wilkins. Together, they helped New York reel off a string of playoff appearances that started with the 1987–88 season and continued throughout the 1990s.

Before the 1991–92 season, the Knicks also added a new coach—the legendary Pat Riley, who had guided the Los Angeles Lakers to four NBA championships during the 1980s. Riley stressed a physical style of play, and the Knicks quickly developed a reputation for toughness. Opposing players often feared for their safety when they drove toward the New York basket. Riley's Knicks finished near the top of the NBA standings each of his four years in New York, reaching the Eastern Conference finals twice and the NBA Finals once in search of another title.

The Knicks came closest to that goal in the 1994 NBA Finals, when they grabbed a three-games-to-two lead over the Houston Rockets and needed just one more victory to claim the crown. It never came. Cold outside shooting, primarily by Starks, and the Knicks' failure to get the ball inside to Ewing in the crunch led to two heartbreaking defeats in Houston.

INTRODUCING...

BERNARD KING

POSITION FORWARD
HEIGHT 6-FOOT-7
KNICKS SEASONS 1982–87

BERNARD KING SPENT NEARLY HALF OF HIS

KNICKS CAREER ON THE SIDELINES, REBUILDING

A SHATTERED KNEE SUFFERED LATE IN JANUARY

1985. But when he was on the court, King was one of the

most exciting offensive talents ever to wear a Knicks uniform.

A two-time All-Star while in New York, King was nearly impos-

sible to defend. In a 1984 first-round playoff series against the

Detroit Pistons, he averaged more than 40 points per game,

despite having dislocated fingers on both hands and suffering

from the flu. The key to King's success was his ability to slash

by defenders for quick jumpers or spectacular dunks. "Ber-

nard has an incredibly explosive first step to the basket," said

his coach, Hubie Brown. King also had the uncanny ability to

get his shot off while on the way up, before defenders could

block it. King never stopped working, even when he was

injured. He underwent two years of painful rehab, determined

to continue his Knicks career. When he walked on the court

again late in the 1986–87 season, New York fans gave him a

four-minute standing ovation.

THE 1994 NBA FINALS BETWEEN THE KNICKS AND HOUSTON ROCKETS FEATURED SOME BIZARRE HAPPENINGS, ON AND OFF THE COURT. The widely publicized series pitted two veteran centers against each other—Patrick Ewing of the Knicks versus Hakeem Olajuwon of the Rockets—neither of whom had ever led his team to a league championship. The clubs split the first two games in Houston and the next two in New York. Then, in Game 5 (a Knicks victory), basketball fans divided their attention between the contest at Madison Square Garden and real-time news coverage of a Los Angeles police chase involving retired football great O. J. Simpson, who was suspected of a double murder. New York dropped the final two games in Houston to end Ewing's championship hopes. Much of the blame fell on the shoulders of guard John Starks. Always a streaky shooter, Starks led a Knicks comeback in Game 6, only to miss a last-second three-pointer that would have ended the series. Then, in Game 7, Starks put up shot after shot but clanked 16 of 18 off the rim in a devastating 90–84 loss.

THE END OF AN ERA

Riley left New York in June 1995 to take over as coach of the Miami Heat and was eventually replaced by his long-time assistant, Jeff Van Gundy. New general manager Ernie Grunfeld rebuilt the club's roster before the 1996–97 season, bringing in forwards Larry Johnson and Buck Williams and guards Allan Houston and Chris Childs to surround Ewing. Guard/forward Latrell Sprewell and highflying center Marcus Camby were later added to the team's mix.

This new cast put together an amazing run in the 1999 playoffs. In the first round, New York shocked the top-seeded Heat on a last-second basket by Houston, clinching a win in the deciding Game 5. The Knicks then wiped out the Atlanta Hawks in the next round before challenging the Indiana Pacers in the Eastern Conference finals.

Swingman Latrell Sprewell averaged nearly 18 points per game during his Knicks career, entertaining fans with many breakaway dunks.

T hings looked bleak when Ewing was lost to a season-ending injury in the second game against Indiana. But the Knicks rallied, just as they had done in 1970 when Willis Reed went down. Johnson completed a miraculous, game-winning, four-point play at the end of Game 3, and the Knicks rode that momentum to defeat the Pacers in six games. Unfortunately, New York's magical run halted in the NBA Finals when the San Antonio Spurs proved too powerful for the under-manned Knicks.

A conference finals defeat in the 2000 playoffs convinced Knicks management that it was time to shake things up by trading away Ewing. The center's departure after 15 years in New York was an emotional one. "Patrick is a champion, even if he hasn't won a championship yet," said Coach Van Gundy. "He practiced and played like a champion each day he was here." With Ewing gone to the Seattle SuperSonics, the Knicks "went small," implementing a new offense based on the outside shooting and inside slashing of Houston, Sprewell, and Camby. The team scratched its way into the playoffs for the 14th consecutive year but fell quickly to the Toronto Raptors in the first round.

When the Knicks got off to a shaky 10–9 start in 2001–02, Coach Van Gundy suddenly resigned, and the team seemed to fall apart, finishing with a dismal 30–52 record. Following the season, management acted quickly and perhaps recklessly, trading Camby to the Denver Nuggets for All-Star center/forward Antonio McDyess, who had great talent but a long history of injuries. The gamble failed when McDyess hurt his knee during a preseason game and was lost for the entire year. Without a solid presence in the middle, the Knicks endured another sub-.500 campaign.

What followed was a series of decisions that most New York basketball fans would look back on with horror. First, team president Scott Layden was fired by club owner James Dolan and replaced by Isiah Thomas, an outstanding former NBA player with only a mediocre record as a coach and administrator. But Dolan was sure that Thomas was a good choice. "Isiah is one of the most celebrated figures in the history of the NBA, and we believe he is the right person to lead this team into the future and deliver a championship-caliber team to all Knicks fans," Dolan said.

Thomas immediately began wheeling and dealing. First, he traded several players and draft picks to acquire point guard Stephon Marbury to lead the New York offense. The arrival of Marbury, a New York high school legend, excited local fans but made them anxious, too. Although he was an expert at breaking down opposing defenses with his quickness, Marbury had a reputation for being selfish, and fans questioned whether he would be able to jump-start the stalled Knicks offense and get the team back on the winning track.

Thomas brought in Hall of Fame coach Lenny Wilkens to run the club on the floor and followed with more player trades. Nearly the entire roster had changed over by season's end. Despite the chaos, Marbury pushed the Knicks into the 2004 playoffs with a 39–43 record, though they were quickly eliminated by the rival New Jersey Nets in the first round. Still, New York fans were optimistic about the team's chances to regain its winning touch.

COURTSIDE STORIES

HEATING UP

Allan Houston beats the Heat defense for an easy layup.

DURING THE LATE 1990S, THERE WAS NO NBA RIVALRY MORE INTENSE THAN THAT BETWEEN THE KNICKS AND THE MIAMI HEAT. The enmity heated up when Knicks coach Pat Riley decided to leave New York and take over the Heat. The two clubs memorably squared off in three consecutive postseason series. In 1997, the favored Knicks held a three-games-to-one series lead when Knicks guard Charlie Ward and Heat forward P. J. Brown tussled near the end of Game 5. When several Knicks stars came off the bench to join the fight, they earned one-game suspensions, and the short-handed Knicks lost the remaining games of the series. The next year, another fight broke out between the two clubs during a first-round playoff battle. This time, 5-foot-7 Knicks coach Jeff Van Gundy jumped in between several giants on the court to break up the fight and avoid suspensions. One year later, the Knicks began their miraculous journey to the 1999 NBA Finals by eliminating the heavily favored Heat on an off-balance driving shot by guard Allan Houston with 0.5 seconds left on the clock.

PATRICK EWING

POSITION CENTER
HEIGHT 7 FEET
KNICKS SEASONS 1985–2000

PATRICK EWING WAS FORTUNATE TO HAVE

STRONG, BROAD SHOULDERS, BECAUSE FOR

NEARLY 15 YEARS, THE 7-FOOT CENTER HAD TO

CARRY THE KNICKS FRANCHISE ON HIS BACK.

From the time he was selected as the number-one overall pick in the 1985 NBA Draft, Ewing was expected to guide the Knicks back to championship glory. Most of those years,

he was asked to lead the team to victory with only a mediocre supporting cast. Still, he continued to score, rebound, and block shots at a team-record pace. And he helped turn the franchise into one of the most competitive and financially successful teams in the league. Before Ewing arrived on the scene, the Knicks seldom filled the seats in Madison Square Garden. But the big man's presence revived New

Yorkers' interest in pro basketball, and the team performed before standing-room-only crowds every home game for nine straight seasons. The Knicks won more than 71 percent of those contests, too. In February 2003, Ewing's number 33 jersey was retired by the Knicks. Five years later, he was inducted into the Basketball Hall of Fame.

CHAPTER FIVE

RUNNING AND RELOADING

The high hopes faded quickly. Thomas continued to tinker with the Knicks' roster over the next three seasons, but nothing seemed to work. He made some questionable trades for players such as center Eddy Curry, forward Zach Randolph, and guards Jamal Crawford and Steve Francis—all high-priced athletes whose long-term contracts caused the Knicks' payroll to exceed the league salary cap and restricted the team's ability to sign free agents. Thomas also fired Wilkens midway through the 2004–05 season and replaced him the following year with veteran coach Larry Brown. But the Knicks were mired in a losing cycle from which they couldn't seem to escape. Thomas and Brown quarreled openly throughout 2005–06, and Dolan was compelled to dismiss Brown, even though the coach had several years remaining on his expensive contract. Dolan then insisted that Thomas himself coach the team he had constructed and turn its fortunes around quickly if he wanted to keep his job.

Just 24 years old, aggressive center Eddy Curry emerged as a centerpiece of the Knicks' offense in 2006–07, leading the team in scoring.

When the Knicks got off to a slow start in 2006–07, chants of "Fire Isiah" began to resound in Madison Square Garden. Then Curry and Marbury keyed a mid-year winning streak, and Dolan decided to extend Thomas's contract despite the opposition of local fans and sportswriters. Thomas would last through one more disappointing season before he, too, was fired and replaced by Donnie Walsh as president and Mike D'Antoni as coach prior to the 2008–09 season.

The new team leaders had some key decisions to make about the club's style of play and its roster. D'Antoni, who had previously built the Phoenix Suns into a Western Conference "run-and-gun" powerhouse, wanted to establish an up-tempo offense in New York as well. "Our goal is to shoot within seven seconds or less," said D'Antoni, "to get a shot up before opponents can react." With that in mind, Walsh and D'Antoni replaced Marbury with former Chicago Bulls point guard Chris Duhon, a "pass-first, shoot-later" guard. They also decided to bench Curry and trade away several slower players for speedy forward Al Harrington and shooting guard Larry Hughes.

D'Antoni combined these players with three young stars who had been drafted or acquired by Thomas: power forward David Lee, an aggressive rebounder who loved to drive to the basket; undersized guard Nate Robinson, whose uncanny leaping ability enabled him to elevate and dunk over much taller players; and small forward Wilson Chandler, an excellent outside shooter. All three became key players on the team that D'Antoni put on the floor during the 2008–09 season.

It took a few months for the players to adapt to each other and to the coach's style, but the "new" Knicks slowly began to improve as the season progressed. More importantly, the team's increased hustle and enthusiasm attracted New York basketball fans back to Madison Square Garden, where cheers replaced the boos of previous seasons. Although the team finished 2008–09 and 2009–10 with losing marks of 32–50 and 29–53, respectively, fans continued to have high hopes for the retooled squad's eventual success.

For more than 60 years, the New York Knicks have lived up to founder Ned Irish's vision of "a first-class team in a first-class city." Loyal New York fans who witnessed the valiant efforts of Willis Reed in the 1970s and Patrick Ewing in the 1990s have come to expect that kind of excellent basketball in Madison Square Garden. With a new coach and a new playing style, today's Knicks plan to deliver.

Although David Lee (opposite) left New York in 2010, the coaching of Mike D'Antoni (below) and acquisition of forward Amar'e Stoudemire—a former Suns All-Star—had Knicks fans thinking big.

INDEX